Short Stack Editions | Volume 12

Brown Sugar

by Libbie Summers

Short Stack Editions

Publisher: Nick Fauchald
Creative Director: Rotem Raffe
Editor: Kaitlyn Goalen
Copy Editor: Abby Tannenbaum
Business Manager: Mackenzie Smith

ISBN 978-0-9907853-1-6

Printed in New York City
October 2014

Table of Contents

Sweets

Drinks

November and December, which contain some of the biggest cooking holidays, are two of our favorite months. Something about the season permits us to take our time, whether it's spending a whole day in the kitchen in the service of one delicious meal or staying at the table with friends just a little bit longer.

Libbie Summers cooks for these sorts of moments. A colorful storyteller, she creates recipes that are so much more than a set of instructions. They meander through tradition and personal experience, capturing the conversations they prompted at her table while encouraging her audience to linger around the stove long enough for new memories to form.

Brown sugar is an ideal conduit for Libbie's approach. The gentle-yet-dynamic sweetener is hidden in plain sight, a fixture in every cupboard. Her recipes demand that we spend more time with this staple and—through recipes such as Nordic caramelized potatoes, her grandmother's ham and brown sugar roasted chickpeas—learn to appreciate what's right in front of us.

—*The Editors*

Introduction

"I don't give a damn 'bout my reputation."

If I'd just listened to Joan Jett and the Blackhearts, I might never have loved brown sugar—the sugar with the cooler reputation.

For a brief second in high school, I thought I needed a better reputation. Questionable choices with boys and booty-short attire had me longing for and in great need of a "do-over." This was also the same time I started my lifelong love affair with brown sugar. It began with the first recipe I ever developed, Jailhouse Cookies. I was 15, full of bravado and thought my play on the traditional Toll House cookie recipe was so clever. Jailhouse Cookies consisted of brown sugar and butter creamed together with a little flour to stiffen the dough and make it easier to stir in a ton of chocolate chips. With the added rich flavor of brown sugar, I told my 15-year-old self that vanilla would be overkill. And, since I ate the dough raw (jailhouse-style), no other ingredients were needed. Those Jailhouse Cookies rocked.

In my late 20s, I accepted my first professional cooking gig aboard a large chartered sailboat in the Caribbean. When I wasn't at the cooking whim of celebrities and celebrity wannabes on charter sails, I found my way to the side of one island road or another, where I sat and chewed the fat—and sugarcane—with the locals. I learned about cutting off the woodsy outer part of the cane and getting to the center, where the sweet sap lies. I learned there's a lot of spitting and laughing, and I learned that my teeth would rot if I kept up this sugarcane habit. It was on St. Kitt's that I spent a day touring a sugarcane farm to see how the cane is harvested and milled to produce turbinado sugar. I watched as the fresh cane was crushed and the first juice expressed. Then the juice was heated to extract the water, leaving big crystals that were spun in a huge turbine to produce light brown sugar, which had a faintly woodsy, caramel flavor. At the end of that memorable day, I enjoyed a cup of tea, sweetened by the farm's turbinado sugar, with the farm workers. It remains the best cup of tea I have ever consumed.

So that's how my appreciation for brown sugar took shape: a batch of cookies, a farm tour and a single cup of tea. Since then, I've cooked with people all over the world, using all types of brown sugars: mostly refined (modern light and dark brown sugar), some partially refined (turbinado and demerara) and a couple of unrefined ones (muscovado and piloncillo).

The recipes I share in this book all have two things in common: a rich flavor thread that runs from savory to sweet, from the appetizers through the desserts, and inspiration from the cast of caramelized characters who've touched my life while teaching my taste buds, from a chickpea vendor on the street in Egypt to a Mexican baker (who I wish had been just a little sweeter). My exploration of brown sugar has taught me to smile a lot, cringe a little and never worry about having a good reputation.

—*Libbie Summers*

Recipes

About Brown Sugar

You'll find a few different varieties of brown sugar in these recipes, depending on the variety, molasses is either added back to refined white sugar (as in modern light or dark brown sugar) or left intact with the sugar crystals during the refining process. Various brown sugars differ primarily by how much molasses each contains. Each sugar has its own distinct flavor, and I encourage you to try experimenting with different brown sugars in all your recipes.

Demerara Sugar

Demerara sugar is made by pressing sugarcane, then steaming the juice of the first pressing. This steaming forms a thick cane syrup. The syrup is allowed to dehydrate, which leaves behind large, pale amber sugar crystals that have a slight toffee flavor.

Turbinado Sugar

Turbinado sugar is a slightly refined sugar made by crushing freshly cut sugarcane to squeeze out the juice, which is then evaporated and spun in a turbine to produce the large, light-brown crystals. Turbinado sugar has a mild caramel flavor, with a texture that is finer and less sticky than demerara sugar.

Muscovado Sugar

Muscovado sugar is coarse, unrefined dark brown sugar. It's moist and has a strong molasses flavor.

Piloncillo (pee-lon-SEE-yoh) Sugar

Piloncillo sugar is made by boiling cane juice down to a thick crystalline syrup. The syrup is then poured into cone-shaped molds to harden. It has a smoky, earthy flavor with a little acidic kick and can be used as a sweetener or a spice.

Light Brown Sugar

Light brown sugar is made by adding a small about of molasses to refined white sugar, which results in a moist sugar with a rich caramel flavor. (To make your own, add 1 tablespoon of molasses to 1 cup of white sugar and mix with a fork or your hands until fully combined.)

Dark Brown Sugar

Dark brown sugar is made by adding a greater amount of molasses to refined white sugar than is required to make light brown sugar. The result is a dark brown, very moist sugar with a rich molasses flavor. (To make dark brown sugar, add 2 tablespoons of molasses to 1 cup of white sugar and mix with a fork or your hands until fully combined.)

Sweet Roasted Chickpeas

The first time I tasted roasted chickpeas was alongside a busy road in Cairo. They were scooped warm from a skillet into a makeshift paper cone by an elderly vendor wearing a sparkling *galabeya* and an infectious smile. This recipe is an homage to that vendor and his chickpeas: earthy, spicy and sweet, with a crunchy coating and a soft middle.

One 15-ounce can chickpeas

1 tablespoon light brown sugar

Pinch ground cayenne

Pinch ground cinnamon

Pinch ground cumin

1 teaspoon kosher salt

1 tablespoon vegetable oil

makes 2 cups

Preheat the oven to 400°. Line a rimmed baking sheet with a silicone baking mat or parchment paper.

Drain the chickpeas in a large strainer and rinse well. Spread the chickpeas out on a kitchen towel or paper towels and pat them dry. (At this point, some of skins may be coming off the beans. You can remove them all if you like. I'm not married to either way.)

Spread the dry chickpeas out on the baking sheet and roast for 15 minutes. Meanwhile, in a small mixing bowl, stir together the brown sugar, cayenne, cinnamon, cumin and salt. Set aside.

Remove the chickpeas from the oven and drizzle with the vegetable oil, turning to coat with a large spoon. Sprinkle the sugar mixture over the chickpeas and mix well, rolling them around the pan until all the peas are coated. Return to the oven and roast for another 15 minutes, stirring every 5 minutes. Turn off the oven, crack open the oven door and leave the chickpeas inside for another 15 minutes. Remove from the oven (the chickpeas will still be slightly soft in the middle). Serve immediately, as the chickpeas do not keep well.

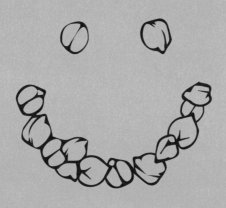

My secret for keeping brown sugar fresh

I make only two cups at a time. For some reason, two cups is the magic number to have on hand. You'll have what you need for a recipe and the rest will keep fine in an airtight container stored in the freezer. Once thawed (and it won't take long with only two cups), the brown sugar will be ready to use.

Salted Brown Sugar Peanut Brittle

With a few notable exceptions (including the best fried chicken I've ever had), my stylish paternal grandmother, Annie Mae, wasn't a particularly gifted cook. Her peanut brittle was notoriously dangerous, and could not be chewed without risking injury. (On two occasions, chewing involved an emergency trip to the dentist with my tooth chip in hand.) I've never seen Annie Mae's recipe, but I'm guessing it didn't involve baking soda, which creates the air bubbles needed to prevent dental emergencies. Each time I make this crunchy sweet brittle, I'm reminded of my beautiful grandmother, how very much I loved her, and her aptitude for fashion over cooking.

---

4 tablespoons unsalted butter, plus more for buttering the pan

½ cup dark brown sugar

1½ cups granulated sugar

1 cup light corn syrup

3 cups unsalted roasted peanuts

2 teaspoons baking soda

½ teaspoon flaky sea salt (I use Maldon)

makes **3** cups

Lightly butter a rimmed baking sheet and set aside.

In a large skillet over high heat, stir together the sugars, the corn syrup and ½ cup of water. Allow the mixture to come to a full boil (about 5 minutes). Stir in the nuts and cook, stirring, until the syrup thickens and turns a slightly darker color and you begin to smell the nuts cooking, about 5 minutes.

Remove from the heat and stir in the baking soda. Working quickly, stir in the 4 tablespoons of butter and continue to stir until the butter has completely melted. Turn the brittle out onto the prepared baking sheet. Working quickly, use the back of your spatula to spread the mixture out to a thin rectangle (about ¼- to ½-inch thick). Sprinkle the top with sea salt. Allow the brittle to cool completely (this should take about 20 minutes) before breaking it into shards and storing in an airtight container. The brittle will keep for a week.

Cracker Jerks

Green handsaw. Pink sword. Gold pistol. What prison inmate thought up these toys for Cracker Jacks, anyway? As a kid, I'd devour box after box of the crunchy caramel-coated popcorn snack, all the while questioning what kind of person came up with this "surprise inside" marketing plan. Then one day, Cracker Jacks became cool. Suddenly, my "surprise inside" was a small book of temporary tattoos, a kid's very definition of awesome. This recipe for my grownup version has a rich, crunchy, deep molasses flavor, as well as its own "surprise inside"—a hint of cayenne to finish each bite. The kick doesn't linger—it stays around about as long as that first temporary tattoo stayed on my skin.

---

3 tablespoons vegetable oil

½ cup popcorn kernels

1 cup Spanish peanuts, husks removed (available in most grocery stores)

1 cup light brown sugar

½ cup corn syrup

4 tablespoons unsalted butter

¼ teaspoon cayenne pepper

½ teaspoon salt

makes **10** cups

Preheat the oven to 250°. In a medium saucepan with a tight-fitting lid, add the oil and 2 popcorn kernels. Cook over high heat until the kernels pop, then add the remaining popcorn, cover and lower the heat to medium-high. Cook until the kernels stop popping, shaking the pan often. Discard any unpopped kernels and spread out the popcorn on a large, deep, nonstick, rectangular cake pan or lasagna casserole dish (I use a 14-by-10-by-4-inch nonstick cake pan). If you use a pan that isn't nonstick, grease it with butter or nonstick cooking spray first. Toss the popcorn with the peanuts and place the pan in the preheated oven to keep warm.

Attach a candy thermometer to the side of a medium sauce-pan over medium heat and add the brown sugar, corn syrup, butter, cayenne pepper and salt. Stir until the mixture comes to a boil. Allow the mixture to cook until the temperature of the candy reaches 260° to 275° on the candy thermometer, about 15 minutes.

Working quickly, remove the popcorn and peanuts from the oven and pour the hot syrup mixture in a fine stream over the popcorn to cover it evenly. Using a nonstick spatula, carefully toss to coat. Return the pan to the oven for 10 minutes, mixing every couple of minutes to evenly coat the popcorn and peanuts. Remove the pan from the oven and let the mixture cool to room temperature before storing in an airtight container. The Cracker Jerks will keep for up to 10 days.

Note: 1 tablespoon of popcorn kernels yields just over 1 cup of popped corn.

Warning: Don't even try this with bullshit microwave popcorn.

Stir-Fried Bitter Greens with Brown Sugar Vinegar

This recipe is great with any mixture of "stiff" greens (dandelion, mustard, collard or kale). The brown sugar vinegar is the perfect finishing touch, as it adds a sweet-and-sour counterpart to the bitter bite of the greens. For a variation, I've been known to add cooked orzo, flaked poached salmon or roasted chicken pieces to the wok before drizzling with the vinegar.

2 tablespoons canola oil

2 cups shredded red cabbage

2 cups ribbon-cut (¼-inch thick) turnip or mustard greens

2 cups ribbon-cut (¼-inch thick) collard greens

2 teaspoons toasted sesame oil

Flaky sea salt

Brown Sugar Vinegar (recipe follows)

serves -4-

Heat a wok or a nonstick skillet over high heat until very hot, then add the canola oil and heat it until it shimmers (I know it seems like a lot of oil, but it's not). Add the cabbage and cook, stirring, for 2 minutes. Stir in the greens and stir-fry another few minutes, until the greens are just starting to wilt. Stir in the sesame oil and liberally salt the greens. Drizzle with a tablespoon or two of Brown Sugar Vinegar and serve immediately.

Brown Sugar Vinegar

1 cup unfiltered apple cider vinegar

2 tablespoons dark brown sugar

½ teaspoon red pepper flakes

makes 1 cup

In a small saucepan over medium heat, add all the ingredients and cook just until the brown sugar has dissolved. Remove the pan from the heat and let the mixture cool for 20 minutes. The vinegar will keep refrigerated for up to 1 month in an airtight container or lidded jar.

Roasted Cauliflower Soup with Sweet Chile Sauce

The sweet chile sauce that punctuates this soup came into my life when I was in college and failing Chemistry for Engineers. The Laotian teacher's assistant who was trying to help me pass taught me how to make it. He served it drizzled atop thick home-made noodles swimming in chicken broth when we took a lunch break during one torturous tutoring session before the final exam. I couldn't stop thinking about how the sweet hot sauce heightened the flavor of the earthy noodles, and I couldn't wait to try it with other soups. Later, I paired it with this earthy, coconut-fueled cauliflower soup, and the result was far more revelatory than anything I learned in that class.

For the soup:

1 large head cauliflower, cut into large florets

2 shallots, quartered

3 garlic cloves, smashed

2 stalks celery (with leaves), cut in half

3 tablespoons vegetable oil

1 tablespoon light brown sugar

Kosher salt and freshly ground black pepper

Vegetable stock, as needed to thin the soup (maximum 2 cups)

One 13.5-ounce can unsweetened coconut milk

For the chile sauce:

2 serrano chiles, finely diced

1 garlic clove, minced

2 tablespoons rice wine vinegar

2 tablespoons soy sauce

2 tablespoons light brown sugar

2 tablespoons honey

serves ·4·

Preheat the oven to 400°. Add the cauliflower, shallots, garlic and celery to a roasting pan and toss with the oil, brown sugar, 1½ teaspoons salt and ½ teaspoon pepper. Roast for 1 hour or until the cauliflower is fork-tender and the vegetables are beginning to brown.

While the vegetables are roasting, prepare the sauce. In a small mixing bowl, stir together the chiles, garlic, vinegar, soy sauce, sugar and honey, and set aside. (Sweet Chile Sauce will stay fresh for 10 days when stored in an airtight container and refrigerated.)

Remove the vegetables from the oven and let cool for a few minutes. Working in 2 batches, place half of the vegetable mixture in a blender and puree with ¾ cup vegetable stock until smooth (if the mixture is too thick, you may need to add more stock to the blender). Pour the first batch into a saucepan and repeat this process with the remaining half of the vegetable mixture.

Place the saucepan with the cauliflower puree over medium heat, add the coconut milk and stir until heated through. For thinner soup, add more of the vegetable stock. Season with salt and pepper to taste. To serve, ladle the soup into bowls and garnish with a drizzle of the sauce.

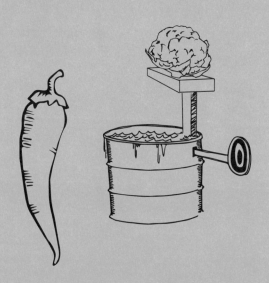

Caramelized Potatoes

I once dated a Danish boy who always smelled of cooked sugar. It wasn't until one particular Christmas—too far from home—when I tasted his mother's sugar-browned potatoes that the boy's scent started to make sense. This is my take on the classic Scandinavian dish. It's a richer, creamier, brown sugar–flavored version, and, although it's finished off with ribbons of earthy sage and almost too much salt, it still smells as sweet as the Danish boy.

12 new potatoes (about 1½ to 2 pounds)

½ teaspoon sea salt

3 tablespoons light brown sugar

2 tablespoons butter

3 tablespoons heavy cream

3 large sage leaves, finely chopped

Flaky sea salt

serves -4-

Place the potatoes and enough water to cover them in a large saucepan and add the ½ teaspoon of salt. Bring to a boil over medium-high heat, then lower the heat to medium and continue cooking until the potatoes are fork-tender, about 8 to 10 minutes, depending on their size. Drain the potatoes and let them cool. When they're cool enough to handle, peel them and discard the skins. Set aside.

In a large skillet over medium-low heat, sprinkle the brown sugar evenly over the bottom of the pan. Cook, stirring, until the sugar completely melts. Stir in the butter and cook just until the two are combined. Increase the heat to medium and add the cream. Cook, stirring continuously, until the mixture starts to thicken. Add the potatoes and stir to coat. Continue cooking, stirring often, until the potatoes are fully coated and start to get a little crisp in spots from the brown sugar, about 6 minutes. (The butter will separate from the sugar after a few minutes —and that's okay!)

Sprinkle the potatoes with the sage and some salt. Transfer to a serving bowl and serve warm. If you have any leftovers, use them the next morning for breakfast, quartered and tossed in a skillet with bacon and scallions and served with eggs.

Butter Lettuce with Brown Sugar & Bacon Dressing

Can a salad be comfort food? Yes, if it's this one. This salad contains everything I love—smoky bacon, crisp greens, warm eggs, a brown sugar–laced dressing and creamy, pungent blue cheese. Basically, it's a hug, a kiss, a rainbow and a puppy all on one 6-inch plate.

2 heads butter lettuce

2 eggs

4 slices thick-cut bacon, diced

2 tablespoons finely chopped sweet onion, such as Vidalia

2 garlic cloves, minced

½ cup red wine vinegar

¼ cup light brown sugar

1 teaspoon Dijon mustard

Kosher salt and freshly ground black pepper

1 avocado, sliced

2 hearts of palm, thinly sliced

Four ¼-inch slices of good blue cheese

serves
·4·

Wash and dry the lettuce, then trim the root ends and halve the heads lengthwise.

In a medium saucepan, cover the eggs with cold water. Cook over medium-high heat until boiling. Boil for 2 minutes, then remove the pan from the heat and let the eggs sit in the water for 10 minutes. Pour out the hot water and replace it with cold water and let the eggs sit for a couple of minutes before peeling them. Once the eggs are peeled (don't worry how bad they look), slice or roughly chop them. (Timing is important with this salad; I think it's best when the eggs are just ever so slightly warm when they're placed on top of the greens, so have them cooking while you're making the dressing.)

In a small skillet over medium heat, add the bacon and cook, stirring occasionally, until crisp and browned, about 8 minutes. Transfer the bacon to a paper-towel-lined plate; leave the drippings in the pan. Add the onion and garlic and cook until the onion is translucent, about 5 minutes. Stir in the vinegar, brown sugar and mustard (make sure to scrape up the bacon bits from the bottom of the pan). Season with salt and pepper to taste. Cook just until the sugar has completely dissolved and the dressing starts to simmer. Remove the skillet from heat and stir in half of the reserved bacon.

Place half a head of lettuce on each of 4 plates. Divide the warm eggs, avocado and hearts of palm evenly among the 4 plates (I like to let the toppings fall in between the leaves of the greens). Drizzle each salad with slightly warm dressing and top with a slice of blue cheese. Garnish each with the remaining reserved bacon. Serve immediately.

Brown Sugar-Pickled Slaw

Hospitality tip: I urge you to make a few batches of this pickled slaw so each of your dinner guests can take a pint home. Let them know it's the perfect topping for softly scrambled eggs for breakfast or piled high on a greasy burger for lunch.

¼ cup dark brown sugar

½ cup rice vinegar

1 teaspoon sea salt

1-inch piece fresh
ginger, peeled and thinly sliced

makes **1** *pint*

1 star anise pod

2 cups finely julienned vegetables
(such as daikon, carrots, cucumber
and red bell pepper)

1 Anaheim chile—stemmed,
seeded and finely julienned

Make this slaw the day before you plan to eat it; in doing so, the slaw can chill and the flavors can blend properly.

In a medium skillet, add ½ cup of water and stir in the brown sugar, vinegar, salt, ginger and star anise. Cook over low heat just until the sugar and salt dissolve. Remove the pan from the heat and set aside to cool.

In a medium bowl, toss the vegetables with the chile. Fill a sterilized pint jar with the vegetable mixture, packing the vegetables in tightly. Pour the cooled brine over the vegetables and tap the jar lightly on the countertop to release any air bubbles. Screw the lid tightly on the jar and refrigerate overnight before using. The slaw will lose its crispness after three days, but the deliciousness lasts for a week.

Seared Brown Sugar-Brined Salmon

I've made this recipe at dinner parties for pastors, pushers and a U.S. president. No matter the chosen vocation, the diner's response has always been the same: "Is there any more of the salmon?" This dish is the perfect combination of flavors: a floral, almost bittersweet flavor from the muscovado sugar enhances the buttery sweet salmon and crunchy sour vegetables. Plus, it's easy to prepare, so you won't be stuck in the kitchen all night with the Secret Service.

1 tablespoon muscovado sugar (dark brown sugar is an acceptable substitute)

1 tablespoon flaky sea salt

¼ cup mirin (Japanese sweet rice wine)

Zest and juice of 2 lemons

2 tablespoons canola or grapeseed oil

Four 6-ounce skin-on salmon fillets

1 pint Brown Sugar–Pickled Slaw (p. 23)

serves
-4-

In a large mixing bowl, stir together 2 cups of warm water, the muscovado sugar, salt, mirin, lemon zest and lemon juice until the sugar and salt have dissolved. Let the mixture cool to room temperature before submerging the salmon in the cooled brine. (I use the leftover juiced lemon rinds to weigh the salmon down and keep it submerged in the bowl.) Cover and refrigerate the salmon for 30 minutes, then remove it from the brine and pat it dry with paper towels. Discard the brine.

Bring a large skillet to nearly smoking over medium-high heat and add the oil. Place the salmon pieces skin side up in the pan and cook for 3 minutes without turning the fillets, or until the opaque color reaches about halfway up the sides of the fillets and the bottom edges are golden brown. (Starting your fish skin side up produces a good sear on the flesh side, while the skin holds the fish together allowing for a clean flip.) Gently turn the salmon over (always away from you) and cook the fillets for another 3 minutes. Transfer the salmon to a paper-towel-lined plate and let the fish rest for 1 minute before serving.

Serve warm, topped with a generous portion of chilled Brown Sugar–Pickled Slaw.

Sticky Toffee Chicken Wings

I first served these messy wings to a group of public school Brits with cheeky attitudes and imperfect smiles. Since there's not much eating sans cutlery across the pond, I thought it would be entertaining to confront my posh guests with a sort of colonist cowboy swagger, then sit back to watch the rodeo. What transpired over the next few hours was one of the most hilariously happy meals I've ever been part of: laughter louder than any fraternity party on game night; sticky toffee sauce from noses to necks; and cleaned chicken bones ending up in places the Territorial Army would never find.

12 chicken wings
(about 3 pounds)

1 cup dark brown sugar

4 tablespoons unsalted butter

⅓ cup lime juice
(about 4 medium limes)

2 tablespoons Sweet Soy Sauce
(page 29; it's okay to substitute regular soy sauce if necessary)

¼ cup Asian fish sauce

1 tablespoon fresh grated ginger

1 jalapeño pepper, thinly sliced, plus more for garnish

makes **24** wings

Preheat the oven to 300°. At the joint separating the drumette from the wingette (or the flat if you live near me in the South), cut each of the chicken wings in half. Cut the tip off each wingette. Set the drumettes and wingettes aside and discard the tips.

In a large oven-safe pan (I use a large ceramic braiser), combine the rest of the ingredients and cook the mixture over low heat, stirring, just until the butter has melted and the sugar has begun to dissolve. Remove from the heat, add the chicken wings and toss to coat. Arrange the chicken wings in a single layer on the bottom of the pan and bake, uncovered, for 1 hour. Increase the temperature to 450° and bake 20 to 25 minutes longer or until the sauce is reduced and the drumettes and wingettes are thickly glazed. During baking, turn the wings a few times so they get a proper gooey coating. Garnish with jalapeño slices and serve warm.

Sweet-and-Sour Pork Chops with Fiery Stone Fruit Sauce

In grilling pork chops, as in life, remember these two very import-ant things: Size and place *do* matter. For the best chops to grill, ask your butcher for a 1- to 1½-inch-thick rib chop cut from the center of the loin. It will have just enough fat to handle the high heat but retain its great flavor. Blade chops (cut from the front of the loin) are likely to be tough, while the loin chops (cut from the opposite end of the loin as the blade chop) tend to dry out over high heat. As for size, keep the chops thick enough to sear on the hottest part of your grill, then push over to the cooler side for the final cooking and basting action.

For the Stone Fruit Sauce:	For the pork chops:
1 habanero chile pepper, seeded if you want less heat	Four center-cut pork rib chops, about 1 to 1½ inches thick
2 cups peeled and diced fresh or frozen peaches (or any other stone fruit)	Kosher salt and freshly ground black pepper
1 tablespoon apple cider vinegar	3 tablespoons muscovado sugar (or other brown sugar)
3 tablespoons dark brown sugar	½ cup apple cider vinegar
1 teaspoon Dijon mustard	¼ teaspoon ground nutmeg
¼ teaspoon ground cumin	3 tablespoons unsalted butter
Kosher salt and freshly ground black pepper	1 teaspoon thyme leaves, plus more for garnish
	Vegetable oil, for the grill

serves
—4—

In a blender, combine all the ingredients for the fruit sauce and pulse until smooth. Season to taste with salt and pepper. Set aside. (You can make the fruit sauce ahead and refrigerate it for up to for 1 week.) Season the pork chops with salt and pepper and set aside at room temperature while you make the sweet-and-sour sauce.

In a small saucepan over medium heat, add the muscovado sugar, vinegar and nutmeg and cook, stirring often, until the mixture starts to thicken a bit, about 5 minutes. Remove from the heat and stir in the butter and thyme. Reserve 2 tablespoons of the mixture and set aside.

Heat a grill with medium-high and low-heat sides and oil the grates. Place the pork chops over the hottest part of the grill and sear until charred on both sides, about 1 minute a side. Move the chops over the low-heat side of the grill and continue cooking and basting with the sweet-and-sour sauce until the internal temperature of the meat registers 135° on an instant-read thermometer placed into the thickest part of the chop. Remove the chops from the grill and let rest at room temperature for 10 minutes before serving.

Drizzle with the reserved sweet-and-sour sauce and top with some of the stone fruit sauce. Garnish with thyme leaves and serve.

Taiwanese Meat Sauce

If the state penitentiary kitchen ran out of chicken-fried steak and mashed potatoes for my final death row meal, I'd request *lu rou fan* (braised pork over rice). Those who have tasted the real deal on one of the many streets of Taipei will understand. For the law-abiding diner who can't make a trip to Taiwan anytime soon, this recipe is perfection: minced pork braised in a rich, sweet soy sauce dotted with shallots and augmented with the distinct flavor of Chinese five-spice seasoning. Consider it a kitchen conjugal visit.

2 teaspoons vegetable oil

1 pound ground pork

⅓ cup fried shallots (you can fry your own in oil or purchase them prepared from an Asian grocery)

¼ cup soy sauce

1 tablespoon Sweet Soy Sauce (recipe follows)

2 tablespoons dark brown sugar

1 teaspoon Chinese five-spice powder

1 tablespoon rice wine vinegar

1 teaspoon black pepper

2 cups pork stock, beef stock or water

4 hard-boiled eggs, peeled

6 cups steamed rice or 1 pound cooked egg noodles

Thinly sliced scallion, for garnish

serves
·4·

Heat the oil in a large skillet over high heat and cook the pork for just 2 minutes, stirring to break up the meat. Stir in the fried shallots, both soy sauces, brown sugar, five-spice powder, vinegar and pepper and cook, stirring constantly, for 1 minute. Add the stock and bring the mixture to a boil. Pierce each of the hard-boiled eggs with the tines of a fork in four places and add to the stock. Cover, reduce the temperature to low and simmer for at least 1 hour (the sauce should still be very thin). Pour the meat sauce over rice or egg noodles, garnish with scallion and serve.

Sweet Soy Sauce

¼ cup plus 2 tablespoons water

1½ cups dark brown sugar

¾ cup soy sauce

makes **1** cup

Add the water to a medium saucepan over medium-high heat, stir in the brown sugar and soy sauce and bring to a boil. Continue to boil about 5 minutes, stirring often, until the mixture thickens to a syrupy consistency. (Make sure to keep an eye on the pot, as the mixture tends to want to boil over. If it does, move the pot away from the heat for a moment to cool down.) Remove the pan from the heat and allow the mixture to cool to room temperature before using. The sauce will thicken as it cools.

The sauce will keep, refrigerated, for 1 week. It's delicious in stir-fry and curry dishes, or try drizzling a little over mashed potatoes (trust me on that one).

Need to get rid of those hard sugar lumps?

Add a moist paper towel to a plastic bag of hardened brown sugar and heat it in a microwave oven in 20-second bursts until the sugar is soft; break up any lumps after each burst (one 20-second burst usually does the trick).

Brown Sugar-Brined Fresh Ham

My hog-farming grandma, Lula Mae, was my swine-cooking sensei. The genius of her hams was in the glaze that complemented the pork's final flavor profile. Sadly, what the glaze added in flavor, it obliterated in texture, causing the once-crispy skin to become a little soggy. In fact, my cousins and I would fight over the crunchy parts that the coating hadn't reached, then dip them into any drippings left in the bottom of the roasting pan. With this brown-sugar-sweetened brine and seasoned rub, I worked hard to achieve the subtle flavor of Grandma's finishing glaze without sacrificing the bonus of a crispy outside—the part I loved most as a kid.

For the brine:

2 cups dark brown sugar

2 cups kosher salt

8 rosemary sprigs

1 tablespoon whole cloves

Four 4-inch cinnamon sticks

1 vanilla bean, split

2 tablespoons red pepper flakes

2 onions, cut in quarters

2 heads garlic, cut in half (no need to remove skins)

One 6-to-8-pound bone-in, skin-on fresh ham (the rear leg of a pig; if you're using only one half of the leg, I prefer the shank end)

For the rub:

4 garlic cloves, minced

¼ teaspoon ground cinnamon

¼ teaspoon ground cloves

¼ teaspoon crushed red pepper flakes

1 tablespoons kosher salt

1 teaspoon coarse ground black pepper

2 tablespoons finely chopped fresh rosemary

½ cup vegetable oil

serves 8 to 10

In a large pot that will fit in your refrigerator, add 2 gallons of water and stir in the brown sugar and salt until both have dissolved. Add the

rosemary, cloves, cinnamon sticks, vanilla sticks and bean, red pepper flakes, onions and garlic and give it a good stir. Place the ham in the brine so it is completely submerged; add more water if necessary. Cover the pot with a lid or plastic wrap and refrigerate for a minimum of 3 days (5 days is my personal sweet spot).

When you're ready to cook the ham, preheat the oven to 450°. Remove the ham from the brine and pat it dry. Discard the brine. Using a sharp knife, score the skin of the ham all the way around in a crosshatch pattern, making sure to cut through only the skin and the fat layer beneath. Set the ham aside while you make the rub.

In a medium bowl, whisk all the rub ingredients into a loose paste. Rub the paste all over the scored ham, getting into each of the scored crosshatches. In a large roasting pan, place the ham on its side and roast for 30 minutes, then remove the pan from the oven and carefully turn the ham over. Return to the oven for another 30 minutes to get the underside nice and crispy.

Reduce the oven temperature to 350° and continue to roast the ham until an instant-read thermometer placed in the ham reaches an internal temperature of 150°, about 1½ hours to 2 hours. Remove the ham from the oven and let it rest at room temperature for 30 minutes before slicing and serving.

Tacos de Carne Asada

I made this dish for a team of Canadian sailors not too long ago. The group silently stared at the festive buffet I'd laid out for dinner. "What is it?" the boat's tactician asked. "How do we eat it?" Once I recovered from the initial shock, it occurred to me that these Canucks were getting really good Mexican food for the first time. They devoured the tacos and have since requested them on two more occasions. I consider this an international victory. The Asada Incident did leave me wondering: Have Mexican sailors ever sampled poutine?

½ cup vegetable oil, plus more for the grill

2 tablespoons grated piloncillo (available at Latin markets; light brown sugar is an acceptable substitute)

4 garlic cloves

Juice of 1 orange (about ⅓ cup)

4 limes, 2 juiced and 2 cut into 6 wedges each

1 chipotle pepper in adobo sauce

½ cup packed chopped cilantro, divided

Kosher salt and freshly ground black pepper

Two 1-pound pieces of trimmed skirt or flank steak

Eight to twelve 7-inch corn tortillas

Queso fresco (available in the dairy section of most grocery stores), crumbled

2 cups prepared pico de gallo or salsa verde

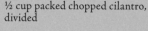

serves
-4-

In a blender, combine the ½ cup of oil along with the piloncillo, garlic, orange juice, lime juice, chipotle pepper and ¼ cup of the cilantro. Process until smooth.

Generously season the steak with salt and pepper and place it in a zip-top plastic bag. Let the steaks marinate at room temperature for 1 hour or in the refrigerator for a maximum of 8 hours.

Heat a grill (or grill pan) to medium-high and oil the grates. Wipe any excess marinade from the steaks and place them on the hot grill. Cook the steaks, turning only once, about 8 minutes a side for medium rare. Transfer the steaks to a cutting board and let them rest for 5 minutes before thinly slicing the meat against the grain.

Warm the tortillas on the grill or in a dry skillet for 30 seconds per side.

Lay a few slices of meat inside a hot tortilla and top with the queso fresco and your choice of pico de gallo or salsa verde. Finish with a squeeze of lime and a sprinkling of cilantro. Repeat with the remaining ingredients and serve.

Sweet-and-Vicious Ribs with Mason Jar Mustard Sauce

There are three things I've been trying to master for the past year. The first: perfecting my dry rib rub recipe. The second: genuinely trying to listen with interest when my friends talk about their newborns. And the third: learning to say "I'm sorry." The rib rub? Nailed it. It's the perfect rub with just the right amount of brown sugar sweetness to tame the big kick of heat from the ground chipotle pepper along with adding an earthy flavor from the molasses and cumin. As for focusing when new moms are talking about their babies? I'm sorry. I've tried. I just can't.

Two 2-pound racks baby back pork ribs

⅓ cup dark brown sugar

1 tablespoon ground cumin

2 teaspoons ground chipotle powder

2 tablespoons paprika

2 teaspoons garlic salt

2 teaspoons flaky sea salt

1 tablespoon coarse black pepper

Mason Jar Mustard Sauce (recipe follows)

serves
·4·

Remove the membrane from the back of each rack of ribs and discard.

In a small bowl, stir together the brown sugar, ground cumin, chipotle powder, paprika, garlic salt, sea salt and pepper. Rub the mixture all over both sides of the ribs, seal them in a large zip-top plastic bag and refrigerator overnight.

Preheat the oven to 250°. Remove the ribs from the bag and wrap each rack individually in a double thickness of heavy-duty aluminum foil. Place the foil-wrapped ribs on a baking sheet and bake in the preheated oven for 2½ to 3 hours or until the meat pulls away from the bones. Remove the ribs from the oven and open the top of the foil just a few inches. Let the meat rest for 15 minutes before cutting the rack into individual ribs. Serve with Mason Jar Mustard Sauce.

Mason Jar Mustard Sauce

¼ cup dark brown sugar

¼ cup cider vinegar

1 tablespoon vegetable oil

1 cup prepared yellow mustard

½ cup honey

½ teaspoon Italian seasoning blend

¼ teaspoon cayenne pepper

Kosher salt and freshly ground black pepper

makes 2 cups

Add the brown sugar and vinegar to a 1-quart Mason jar and shake until the sugar has dissolved. Add the oil, mustard, honey, Italian seasoning and cayenne pepper. Cover and shake until well combined. Add salt and pepper to taste and shake again before using. This sauce will keep, refrigerated, for up to 1 month.

Triple-Threat Ginger Cookies

You know that feeling of bravado you get when you know you've nailed a recipe? You'll certainly have it with this cookie. I guarantee you'll want to sashay—and maybe even strut—whenever you offer up a plate of these brown sugar molasses cookies with not one, not two, but three times the ginger.

2¼ cups all-purpose flour

3 teaspoons ground ginger

1 teaspoon baking soda

¼ teaspoon salt

¾ cup unsalted butter, softened

1 cup packed dark brown sugar

1 egg

¼ cup molasses

1½ tablespoons minced fresh ginger root

½ cup minced crystallized ginger, divided

½ cup turbinado sugar

In a medium mixing bowl, whisk together the flour, ground ginger, baking soda and salt. Set aside.

In a large bowl, using a hand mixer, cream the butter and brown sugar together until smooth. Beat in the egg and molasses. Gradually beat in the flour mixture, then mix in the fresh ginger and ¼ cup of the crystallized ginger. Wrap the dough in plastic and refrigerate for at least 2 hours or up to overnight.

Preheat the oven to 350°. Line a baking sheet with parchment paper.

In a small mixing bowl, stir the turbinado sugar and the remaining crystallized ginger together. Shape the dough into 1½-inch balls and roll them in the turbinado sugar mixture to coat. Place the balls on the baking sheet about 2 inches apart and bake until lightly browned, 10 to 12 minutes. Repeat the process until all the dough has been baked into the cookies. Let the cookies cool, remove from the baking sheet and serve. They will keep in an airtight container for up to 5 days.

Juanita's Capirotada

Each year around Easter I think of Juanita, the third wife of my neighbor Pilar. Juanita was from Mexico and she didn't speak English but was fluent in "judgment." She made the very best version of *capirotada* (a Mexican riff on bread pudding) I'd ever had—better than all the versions I've tried in Mexico. After much pleading, she finally taught me her recipe, with Pilar acting as translator. Juanita believed the ingredients of her *capirotada* symbolized the crucifixion of Christ. The bread: body of Christ. The cinnamon sticks: cross. The raisins: nails on the cross. The piloncillo syrup: blood of Christ. The melted cheese: holy shroud. This is my delicious version of Juanita's recipe...minus the judgment.

One 8-ounce cone piloncillo (available at Latin markets)

One 12-ounce can evaporated milk

4 cinnamon sticks

2 cloves

2 eggs

4 day-old *bolillos* (small, savory Mexican baguettes) or 1 French baguette, sliced into about 24 1-inch slices

Vegetable oil, for frying

8 ounces grated queso Oaxaca or mozzarella

⅔ cup raisins

¼ cup pecans, toasted and roughly chopped

¼ cup peanuts, toasted and roughly chopped

8 tablespoons butter, plus more for the baking dish

serves **6 to 8**

In a medium saucepan over medium-high heat, combine the piloncillo, evaporated milk, ½ cup of water, the cinnamon and the cloves. Bring to a boil, then reduce the heat and simmer until the piloncillo has melted (there will be a little sugar sludge remaining in the bottom of the pan; it's fine to leave it there). Remove the pan from the heat and let the mixture cool completely. Remove the cinnamon sticks and cloves, then whisk in the eggs. Set aside.

In a medium sauté pan over high heat, add enough oil to reach a 1-inch depth and fry each slice of bread until golden brown on both sides. Remove and drain on a paper-towel-lined plate. Set aside.

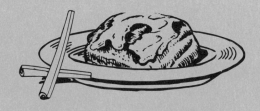

Preheat the oven to 350°. Grease an 8-by-8-inch-deep baking dish with butter. In a medium bowl, combine the grated cheese, raisins and nuts.

Working in layers, like a lasagna (you'll be doing three to four layers), line the bottom of the dish with slices of the fried bread. Top with a sprinkle of the cheese, raisins and nuts. Ladle some of the sweet milk mixture on top. Continue adding layers, ending with the cheese, raisins and nuts. Ladle the last of the milk mixture over the top, then dot with the butter. Cover the baking dish with foil and bake for 10 minutes or until the pudding is bubbling. Remove the foil and continue to bake 10 to 15 minutes longer or until the top is browned. Remove from the oven and allow the pudding to rest for 10 minutes before scooping it into bowls and serving warm.

Brown Sugar Meringue Cookies

Simple, airy, sweet and crunchy, with a mocking sun-kissed hue. If these meringue cookies were people, we probably wouldn't be friends. Sure, I eat a minimum of six of these guilt-free delicious cookies in any given half hour at a posh get-together and love every bite...but hang out with them in a back alley party in the dirty South? Never. Unlike my friends, these cookies are meant to impress with little effort.

4 egg whites, at room temperature

¼ teaspoon cream of tartar

1 loosely packed cup dark brown sugar

½ teaspoon salt

makes **3** dozen

Preheat the oven to 200° and line 2 baking sheets with parchment paper.

In the bowl of a stand mixer fitted with the whisk attachment, whip the egg whites at medium-low speed until foamy. Add the cream of tartar and increase the speed to medium-high, whipping until the whites hold soft peaks. With the mixer running at medium speed, add the brown sugar a little at a time until it is fully incorporated. Increase the speed to medium-high and whip until the meringue holds very stiff peaks.

Spoon the meringue into a pastry bag fitted with a large (½-inch) star tip. Pipe 1½-inch dollops of meringue onto the baking sheets about 1 inch apart. Bake for 1 hour, then rotate the baking sheets and continue to bake for 1 more hour. When the baking time is up, crack the door (I put a wooden spoon in the door to hold it open) and leave the meringues in the oven for a few more hours or overnight to finish drying. Stored in an airtight container, these cookies will stay crisp for up to 1 week.

Bollywood Pudding (Memory Halwa)

My first taste of *halwa*, at an over-the-top Bollywood-ish wedding of a noted Indian businessman, was a revelation. The sweet carrot pudding, a fixture of most Indian celebrations, could be the sole reason these parties are so full of energy: being hopped up on that amount of sugar and love at the same time would keep anyone dancing for hours. This is my version, with less sugar and a more prominent almond flavor than I remember from my first tasting. I made it recently for the same Indian gentleman whose wedding I attended. He offered a few suggestions for tweaking the recipe before getting up from the dinner table and dancing by himself, with his eyes closed and accompanied only by the music of his memory.

1 cup milk

½ cup demerara sugar or light brown sugar

2½ cups firmly packed, coarsely grated carrots (about 7 medium)

1 cup ricotta cheese

½ cup plus 2 tablespoons clarified butter, melted and divided

4 cardamom pods, seeds crushed into a powder (or ½ teaspoon ground cardamom)

⅛ teaspoon freshly grated nutmeg

¼ cup almond paste

10 whole unsalted cashews

8 unsalted pistachios, roughly chopped

12 golden raisins

serves
·4·

In a heavy-bottomed skillet over low heat, combine the milk and sugar and stir until the sugar has completely dissolved. Add the carrots and bring to a simmer. Cook, stirring occasionally, until the carrots are very tender, about 30 to 40 minutes.

Stir in the cheese, ½ cup of the butter, cardamom and nutmeg. Continue cooking, stirring often, until the mixture starts to pull away from the sides of the pan and looks dry, about 30 minutes. Stir in the almond paste, cashews, pistachios, raisins and the remaining butter and cook, stirring, for 2 minutes longer. Divide among bowls and serve hot or warm.

Brown Sugar Pie

I first tasted a version of this Amish pie as a child, sitting around an outdoor table with a bunch of Mennonite kids who lived on the farm next to my grandparents' land. I didn't know then what it meant to be Amish or Mennonite, or how eating this pie crossed those buggy lines of faith. I only knew it was the best pie I had ever eaten, outside of my mother's chocolate cream pie. Today I make this interfaith version—rich and thick sweetness, with a thin crispy layer on top and the flakiest of cinnamon-spiced crusts.

For the crust:

2½ cups all-purpose flour

½ teaspoon kosher salt

1 teaspoon ground cinnamon

12 tablespoons (1½ sticks) cold unsalted butter, cubed

¼ cup lard or vegetable shortening, chilled

For the filling:

2 cups firmly packed dark brown sugar

2 eggs, lightly beaten

1½ teaspoons vanilla bean paste (available at gourmet food markets and online)

4 heaping tablespoons all-purpose flour

6 tablespoons milk

4 tablespoons unsalted butter, melted

Make the crust: In a large mixing bowl, whisk together the flour, salt and cinnamon. Using two forks or a pastry blender, cut in the butter and lard, making sure to leave some chunks of butter the size of peas. Stir in ¼ to ½ cup of ice water—just enough water so that the flour mixture forms a ball. Work quickly and do not overmix. Form the mixture into two equal disks. Cover each with plastic wrap and refrigerate for 2 hours. The dough will be a little crumbly, but that's okay; it will come together when you roll it out. The dough can be refrigerated for up to 2 days or frozen for up to 3 months. This pie recipe calls for a single crust, so freeze the remaining dough to use later.

Preheat the oven to 350°. Roll out the dough on a lightly floured surface, then drape it into a 9-inch pie plate. Trim the dough to leave a ½ inch overhang beyond the edge of the pie plate. Turn the excess dough under itself to create a plumper edge and decoratively crimp the edges. (Be creative here: I've been known to use pearls, corkscrews and tongs to crimp my pies.)

Make the filling: In the bowl of a stand mixer fitted with the whisk attachment, combine the remaining ingredients and beat at medium speed for 2 minutes. Pour the brown sugar filling into the pie shell and bake for 50 minutes or until the pie has set and the crust is browned. Remove the pie from the oven and set aside to cool for 30 minutes to 1 hour before slicing and serving.

Brown Sugar-Scorched Lemonade

There are few things better than sitting on a screened-in porch in the summer while sipping a glass of this lemonade. I think of it as a privilege for those of us lucky enough to live in the South, a reward for surviving the annual sand gnat season. The thing is, our lemons aren't very juicy during the summer months. My solution: "scorching" the lemons in a hot pan before squeezing them, which yields 40 percent more juice and a subtle caramelized flavor.

¾ cup turbinado sugar, divided
(or any light brown sugar)

1 vanilla bean, split

4 lemons, halved

In a small saucepan over low heat, stir together ½ cup of the sugar and 1 cup of water until the sugar has completely dissolved. Remove the pan from the heat, add the vanilla bean and let the vanilla bean steep in the water to taste.

After the pan has cooled, remove the vanilla bean and save it for another use (make vanilla sugar—your baking will never be the same). Note: A faint vanilla flavor is what you are trying to achieve in this sugar syrup.

Pour the remaining ¼ cup of sugar onto a small plate. Dip all the cut sides of the lemons into the sugar to coat the surfaces.

Heat a medium skillet over high heat. Place the sugar-coated lemon halves, sugar side down, in the hot pan and cook for about 30 to 45 seconds or until the sugar starts to turn a dark caramel brown and begins to bubble around the lemons. Remove the pan from the heat and allow it to cool enough so you can handle the lemons easily.

Fill a pitcher with 2 quarts of water. Squeeze the lemons over the pitcher, then drop the squeezed lemons into it. Stir in the vanilla sugar syrup. To serve, fill a glass with ice and pour the lemonade over the cubes.

The James Brown Sugar

I designed a party for a group of New York–based food writers and magazine editors, and this was the specialty drink I created for them. Initially I called it The Badger (long story), but when one particular guest enjoyed a few too many Badgers that night and started working the party like a job, my staff and I quietly changed the cocktail's name to The James Brown Sugar, a nod to the hardest-working man in show business.

1¼ ounces bourbon

¾ ounce Cointreau

1 teaspoon brown sugar

Juice of 1 orange (about 2 ounces)

Juice of ½ lemon (about 1 ounce)

Dash Angostura bitters

Dash blood orange bitters

1 orange twist

makes **1** drink

Fill a pint-size canning jar with ice and add all the ingredients except the orange twist. Screw on the lid and shake well. Remove the lid and twist the orange peel over a glass and drop it into the drink. Add a straw and serve.

Thank You!

---

was a fan of Short Stack editions before I became an author of one. I didn't need *The New York Times* to tell me how nostalgically cool they are, but I'm glad they did so everyone else in the world would know. Thank you to Nick and Kaitlyn for going old-school to create something new-school, and to Rotem Raffe for your cheeky illustrations.

To my talented editor, Janice Shay of Pinafore Press, thank you for always doing the right thing with the curse words and bad grammar that butter my written works. And for making me laugh when you declared (after reading these headnotes) that if personalities were flavors, mine would be "sweet and sour."

A huge thank you to my assistant, Candace Brower, who tested and retested recipes so often her hair smelled of burnt sugar for days. You were an invaluable part of this book and my life for the last year. Thank you for your loyalty, beauty, talent and reduction of Instagram selfies.

Finally, thank you to the sweetest thing I will ever put in my mouth... Josh Summers.

Libbie Summers

Share your Short Stack cooking experiences with us (or just keep in touch) via:

#shortstackeds   facebook.com/shortstackeditions

@shortstackeds   hello@shortstackeditions.com

Colophon

This edition of Short Stack was printed by Circle Press in New York City on Mohawk Britehue Ultra Fuchsia (interior) and Neenah Oxford White (cover) paper. The main text of the book is set in Futura and Jensen Pro, and the headlines are set in Lobster.

Sewn by: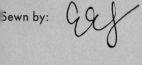

Available now at ShortStackEditions.com:

Vol. 1 | Eggs, by Ian Knauer

Vol. 2 | Tomatoes, by Soa Davies

Vol. 3 | Strawberries, by Susan Spungen

Vol. 4 | Buttermilk, by Angie Mosier

Vol. 5 | Grits, by Virginia Willis

Vol. 6 | Sweet Potatoes, by Scott Hocker

Vol. 7 | Broccoli, by Tyler Kord

Vol. 8 | Honey, by Rebekah Peppler

Vol. 9 | Plums, by Martha Holmberg

Vol. 10| Corn, by Jessica Battilana

Vol. 11| Apples, by Andrea Albin

Vol. 12| Brown Sugar, by Libbie Summers